CHRISTOPHER COLUMBUS & THE AMERICAS: 3RD GRADE US HISTORY SERIES

**Christopher Columbus
was an Italian explorer,
navigator and colonizer.**

SOUTH SEA

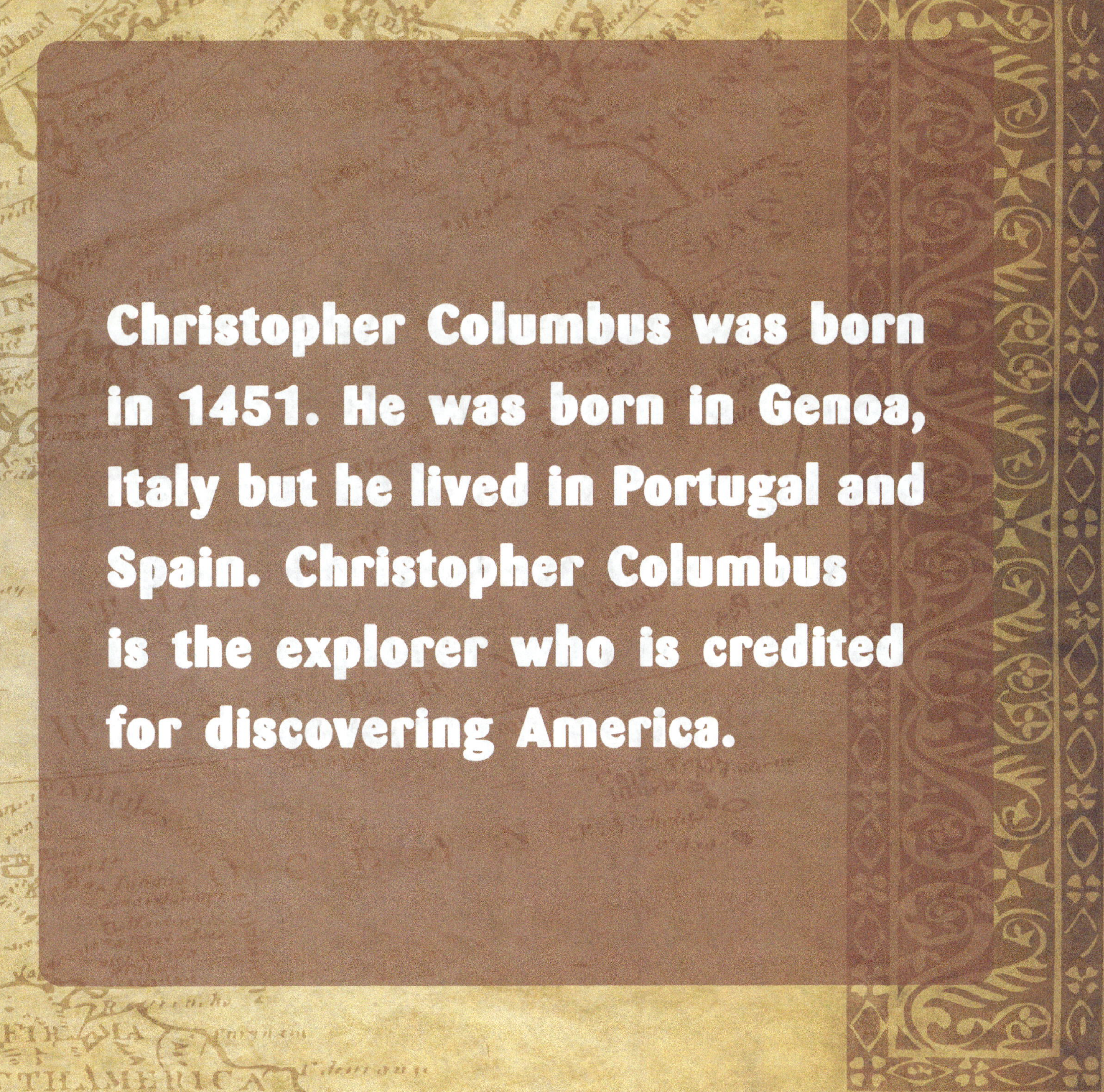

Christopher Columbus was born in 1451. He was born in Genoa, Italy but he lived in Portugal and Spain. Christopher Columbus is the explorer who is credited for discovering America.

He set sail on
August 1492
with three ships
named the Nina,
the Pinta, and
the Santa Maria.

The land was sighted on October 1492.

Christopher Columbus landed on Watling's Island in the Bahamas, West Indies, which he called San Salvador.

He was the first European since the 10th century to have the opportunity to explore the Americas.

He encountered
native peoples
who he named
Indians because
he believed they
were inhabitants
of the Indies.

After his discovery, Columbus was eager to return to Spain and claim his riches. Upon returning home, Columbus was treated like a hero.